# Graduating From College?

## A Practical Guide To Help You Succeed In The Real World

By

**Scott Kenneth Campbell, Ph.D.**

Dear Reader,

     If you have purchased, or had this book purchased for you, the implication is that you either have or soon will be graduating from college. Allow me to offer my congratulations on this momentous accomplishment. A significant proportion of our population at least attempts college. However, the sad reality is that only about twenty percent of the people actually hold it together long enough to graduate. By concentrating on your studies, the sacrifices that you have made, and the efforts you have expended, you have demonstrated to current and future employers that you are someone who will succeed year after year.

     However, now that you have completed or nearly completed your studies, there are certain facts you should be made aware of, and certain advice you should at least be exposed to in order to improve your chances for a prosperous life. Year after year I have students come and talk to me. Most of these students have the same questions, and need the same advice. Within these pages I have enclosed the guidance I have shared with my students for many years. Again, allow me to offer my congratulations and wish you all the success you have worked so hard for.

                        Sincerely,
                        Scott Kenneth Campbell, Ph.D

| Chapter | Page |
|---|---|

# CHAPTER 1
# HOW TO FIND A JOB
♠♠♠♠
## (CAN'T I JUST MOVE BACK HOME)

"Dr. Campbell", my students will say, "I am looking for work." This simple sentence, so elegant in its simplicity is often the beginning step for most college graduates. Having studied and striven for four or five (Or six or seven or....) years you are naturally eager to reap the rewards you have been longing for since your first day of school. However, the choice of one's employment is very often the central decision on your happiness for the next few years. Therefore, several aspects of "I am looking for work" need to be addressed.

DO NOT choose a job based solely on money. That is an easy statement to make when one is not broke, but if you choose a well paying but unpleasant job, you will be unhappy for most of the year. Keep in mind that you will work 8 – 10 hours a day, 5 – 6 days a week for 48 weeks a year. If you add in the time you spend preparing for and getting to work and the time getting home in the evening, you will spend almost all of your waking hours at work or in transit. If the job is unpleasant, if your boss is difficult to work for, if you are bored, stressed, the place smells bad etc, then you will find little enjoyment in your extra income. Remember that with taxes, each additional $5000 in annual salary will really only result in about an extra $10 a day in your pocket. Do you really want to work in a bad job or for an unpleasant supervisor for a lousy extra dollar an hour? If at all possible, find a job you enjoy. There will be plenty of bad days in any job, so do not seek to add to your displeasure.

> *"...recruiters are there to try and sell you on applying to their company."*

Looking for work is rough! You spend years in study, rack up debts, build up dreams, then you find that you are one of close to 700,000 students who graduate every four months in this country and suddenly looking for work is hard. It may help to know that the other 699,999 are also unhappy about their job search, so don't feel too bad. The major mistake you can make in looking for work is to send out dozens of resumes and wait by the phone. A sad fact of life is that with rare exception, most people who are graduating from college have not done enough for their resume to be all that unique. Do not feel bad. In time

2

you will acquire the experience and the skills that will make you stand out a bit. However, try to remember that at least on paper, you probably look very similar to everyone else at the moment.

What can you do to solve this problem? Well, there are several potential answers. First, save your money and don't send resumes to dozens of companies and just wait for an answer. Like much of what is good in life, you will likely have to work hard to land a good job. College job fairs are a good place to start. You will meet some recruiters for various employers. In doing so, you can ask questions about what jobs are available for new college graduates. Recruiters can answer your questions about realistic salaries and working conditions for entry level employment. However, remember that the company recruiters are sales people. As surprising as that may seem, recruiters are there to try and sell you on applying to their company. Therefore, be sure to retain a bit of doubt when you are getting answers to your questions. Do not waste your time looking in the newspapers. Often companies will advertise in newspapers, receive dozens of applications, and hire someone who did an internship there anyway.

If you really want to land a good job fast, pick three or four companies that interest you. Utilize the internet, friends who work there, articles you may find in the paper or in magazines, and research the company or companies you are targeting. When you have settled on three or four companies that your research indicates you may enjoy working for, contact them repeatedly until someone hires you.

> "If your hand writing is poor, have a friend, family member, hire a scribe, whatever, but get that note in the mail the very next day."

I often tell students to just show up at the businesses for which you are hoping to work. Do not go on a Monday, or any mornings for that matter. People do much of the work they will accomplish for the week on Monday. For the rest of the week, people generally do most of a day's work before lunch. Show up after lunch, around 1:30 – 2:00 on a Tuesday or a Wednesday and knock on the door. You will often find people who are fresh from lunch, they do not really want to get back to their work, and talking to you for a bit counts as work.

Always wear professional attire when you are out trying to get an interview with a potential employer. When you get in to see someone, make sure you stress that you are interested in working for their company. Come prepared with good copies of your resume, and have multiple copies in case you get to meet more than one person. DO NOT ask about pay, benefits, working conditions, vacation times etc. while you are in your initial interview. Sometimes the people you are speaking with may offer this information, but never ask. Use the research you have done in identifying the companies you are interested in, and make sure you have some good questions about the company. A good way to start is to stress that you have been researching the company or organization for some time before you came to seek employment. Stress the aspects of the company or organization that caught your attention. Be prepared to ask specific questions about the company's products or services. Be sure to listen to the answers that are given, and stress where your interests lay.

The people you initially speak with will probably not have much time to spend with you, maybe 10 – 15 minutes is all that they will spare. However, unlike everyone else in the resume pile, they now have a face and some memories to associate with your name. No matter how long they speak with you, WRITE A THANK YOU NOTE. I know it is old fashioned, but trust me, write the note. Get some of those "Thank You" cards from the store and hand write the thank you note. If your hand writing is poor, have a friend, family member, hire a scribe, whatever, but get that note in the mail the very next day. You will be surprised how many people managers seriously consider for an entry lever job. A show of interest and a little bit of manners will go a long way towards getting your name to the top of their list.

# CHAPTER 2
# RESUMES AND REFERENCES
# FOR JOB HUNTING

♠♠♠♠

## (THE SAD DEMISE OF HAPPY BUNNY)

Your resume is a source of information for potential employers. Strive to make it as clear as possible for them. Your goal is to keep your resume to one page. References can be placed on a second page. Make sure that your name, mailing address, phone numbers and e-mail address are prominent and correct. That unnecessary sentence about your career goals is a waste of time and you just might put something in there that will detract from the job for which you are applying. Employers know, "You want a job where you can work in a challenging environment with the potential for excitement and advancement." Don't we all? The reality is that at this point, you are willing to take anything with a pay check attached to it, and are probably still uncertain what career path you will follow. Don't worry, we will get to career options at the end, right now lets get you hired someplace.

Always include your references with your resume. That whole, "References available upon request." line is a mistake.

Why would employers spend a few days trying to get references from you when the next person in the resume pile looks as qualified as you on paper, and has references included with their resume?

Employers prefer references who can attest to your potential job performance. Some good candidates for references include some of your college professors, maybe even a high school teacher who was influential in your education. In addition, current or former supervisors make valued references, as well as professional family friends who may have known you for some time. Avoid listing roommates, former sorority or fraternity members, girlfriends or boyfriends, or others close to your age and experience. Their input will be less valued by potential employers.

Before you list anyone as a reference, make sure you ask the person if they would be comfortable giving you a positive recommendation. If they are not comfortable giving you a positive recommendation, learn why, but make sure you do not list them as a reference on your resume. In addition, many people tend to avoid confrontation. Therefore, potential references may tell you that they will give you a good recommendation when their tone, hesitation to agree, or body language may indicate otherwise. If you are unsure of a reference, do not include them on your resume. Trust your instincts, they will usually be correct.

When you have identified a good reference, make sure you get their correct information. On your resume, make sure you include the reference's name, spelled correctly, and any job titles such as, "Professor" or "Manager" that they hold. A great source of their formal title is their business card. Ask for one when you are speaking with them. Make sure you include where they work, and their preferred mailing address. You will need to include a phone number and perhaps a cell phone

> *"...do you really want potential employers to be greeted with some thinly veiled sexual innuendo..."*

number if your reference is out of the office a good deal. In addition, make sure you include a current e-mail address for your reference if possible. Before you begin to submit your resume to potential employers, double check to make sure all information for your references is correct. If more than a few months have passed since you initially spoke to a reference, make sure you contact them to verify that none of your reference's information has changed.

Make sure your e-mail address is professional. When one is applying for a well paying professional job, an e-mail address along the lines of "superstud69@msn.com" or "happybunny@yahoo.com" or an amazing variety of others I have seen over the years are totally inappropriate. Some version of your name is probably the best. For years, mine was "scottcampbell@aol.com". A professional e-mail address that references your name, will allow potential employers to know to whom they have sent the e-mail.

The same advice for professional e-mail addresses holds true for your answering machine and voice mail messages. Silly or inappropriate messages are just fine when your calls are from friends, family or people you gave your number to in a bar. However, do you really want potential employers to be greeted with some thinly veiled sexual innuendo or a bad rendition of a song when they attempt to call you?

A new twist on professional applications is the homepages and similar postings that you may have placed on sites like Facebook or MySpace. I personally know three students of mine who lost out on good jobs because of some of the embarrassing antics or statements they had posted on their sites. Potential employers often search the internet for information about new hires, and they really are not impressed with that lovely shot of you from spring break where your pants were on, but your bra was not. Or that fine shot of you passed out and your friends have posed you with some stuffed animals and liquor bottles and thoughtfully decorated you with every marker in the house. Don't get me wrong, I was in a fraternity and I have some great pictures of me that I only show to the closest of friends.

In summary, put some thought into preparing your resume. You need to make sure it is clean, well written, informative and short. Make sure to address the issues that I have raised in this section. In addition, it never hurts to have a knowledgeable and experienced person, such as one of your professors, review your resume with you.

# CHAPTER 3
# APPROPRIATE ATTIRE
# FOR AN INTERVIEW
♠♠♠♠
## (YOU SHOULD SEE THE OTHER GUY)

There are some students that have an excellent GPA or perhaps several years of work experience which will set them above other applicants applying for their first post college job. If you happen to be Harvard's Valedictorian this year you could probably wear a house robe to an interview and still be offered any job for which you may wish to apply. However, for the other 2.6 million of you who have worked hard and graduated from college, the reality is that on paper most of you look identical. You may have heard the expression, "There is never a second chance to make a good first impression." Right or wrong, you will be judged on your appearance the moment you step through the door. Very often these initial judgments will be the deciding factor on who gets offered the job.

Every semester I have students stress to me that "In their field" or "At this company" no one wears coat and tie to work. They are often correct. In most places of work, employees do wear various degrees of "Business Casual" attire.

During these discussions, I have to remind myself that most of the students I am working with, in fact most of you who are reading this book are in your early twenties. In general, you still have the mindset of trying to blend in and be accepted with "The Others" that so many of us so painfully remember from high school. Ask your parents about some of the wilder styles that were prevalent in their youth. I myself have some "Miami Vice" flashbacks, but I digress.

Whenever this conversation arises, I always stress that you are NOT being compared to the people who already work there. You are being compared to the pile of other applicants who are all

> **"Clothing for Christmas might not be as fun as an iPod..."**

trying to get the job. You are trying to separate yourself from the other applicants, not blend in with them. You can express your originality later, but for the time being, you are seeking employment.

When you step into someone's office for your initial interview, it does not hurt for you to look like an executive with the company. Gentlemen, buy a dark blue suit, white shirt, black shoes and a red tie. If you are not sure of the look, a quick glance at the cover of Forbes, Fortune, or any business magazine should show you what I mean. Ladies, your outfit is not as easy to specify. However, I recommend something conservative and tasteful, preferably in navy blue as well. A trip to any large business, such as a bank or law firm, and reading through the afore mentioned business magazines should provide my female readers with plenty of examples of appropriate attire for the interview process. Remember, you went to college for a reason, do not lose that good starting job solely because you looked like the janitor, and not the boss.

On a regular basis, I have students tell me that they do not have any of the attire that I have recommended for an interview. In these instances I always stress a few points. First, you do not need a $2000 suit to get an entry level job. Most people who have a job don't have a $2000 suit. On the other hand, you really do not want to walk into that interview wearing the "Two pair of slacks and a Jacket for $99.95" outfit. A cheap suit looks cheap, and that is not the image you are trying to project.

"How much should I spend" is always the next question. To which I reply, $500 - $600 will get you a complete very presentable look. Buy one outfit, and keep it separate for job hunting purposes only. Don't wear the shoes to work, the tie to church, the outfit to a wedding etc. The less you wear your interview outfit, the less likely it will be soiled or damaged when you need it. Students ask me all the time how can you tell the difference between a cheap suit and one that I am recommending. If you look at the shoulders, the answers are easy. In a cheap outfit, fabric is conserved so they are often tight across the shoulders and back. In addition, no effort is made to align any pinstripes between the front and back panel or between the sleeves and the body of the suit. Somewhere around $300 - $400 dollars the stripes start to align and the outfit is not cut so tight.

Students often tell me that they just don't have $500 - $600 dollars for an outfit. This is not surprising. Students, like many of us, spend every dollar they have as fast as they get it. To someone who's take home pay is probably $5 dollars an hour, $500 - $600 is going to seem like a lot. I will offer a couple suggestions. If you happen to be graduating in May, a good interview outfit makes a wonderful Christmas present. Clothing for Christmas might not be as fun as an iPod, but it does solve the problem of where to get your wardrobe. In that same vein, if you are fortunate enough to have parents who can and are willing to help you purchase an interview outfit, this does make a fine graduation gift. However, if you are like many students who are supporting themselves, then you may have to just save the money for a few months. As a last resort, either charge your new outfit to your credit card, or if your credit is maxed out get a new card and use it to buy your outfit. I have a hard time recommending that students saddle themselves with high interest debt for clothing. However, a good first impression may very well get you a much better starting job. Just be sure to pay that card off fast.

# CHAPTER 4
# PROFESSIONAL APPEARANCE AT WORK
♠♠♠♠
## (WHERE DO I PUT THE NINTENDO?)

When you start your new job, carefully pay attention to how the people you work with, and more importantly the people you work for dress. You need to accept that the clothing you wore as a college student is not likely to be appropriate for professional attire. At the very least, adopt the attire of the people you work with. However, much like when you were looking for employment, I would caution you against trying to blend in with your fellow coworkers. In almost every professional setting, you will have 5 – 6 employees to one manager. Often, the people you are working with are all competing against you for the next managerial slot. If you blend in, you are less likely to get noticed, and therefore less likely to be promoted quickly.

Observe the style of dress that your manager and upper level managers adopt. If like many people, your goal is to be promoted and advance in your job, adopt the clothing choices of your supervisors. The old expression is, "Dress for the job you want." It is not always going to be easy. First, you will need to make sacrifices to afford a better line of clothing than your salary

17

might easily allow. In addition, since you may not be blending in with your coworkers, you might be subjected to some badgering, and maybe even some outright ridicule. It is not easy to be rejected by some of your coworkers. You are going to have to accept that many of your coworkers are your competition, and will not be your close friends.

However, you will be spending many hours a day, every day for weeks and months on end with your coworkers. Competition aside, you will likely find coworkers who you will genuinely admire and who may very well grow into close friends. Simply by choosing where you work, and the field you work in, you and many of the people you work with will have a lot in common. Make sure you are courteous and friendly to everyone, and be a friend to those who are friendly with you. Why not? Life is too short to cut yourself off from natural friendships.

> *"...supervisors will view your personal expenditures as a sign that you take yourself and your job seriously."*

Make sure you extend your neat and orderly appearance to your work and your workspace. You will probably begin your working career in a cubicle, or even an open desk on the work floor. Make sure you keep your desk, cubicle, office or any other work area neat and organized. When you go to work, you will see examples of both those who maintain an organized working environment, and those who don't. Piles of unfinished work, or work that has been completed but not filed, returned to storage, shredded etc... all conspire to create a working environment that gives the appearance of clutter. Individuals with cluttered workspaces will often tell you, rather smugly, that "It may be cluttered, but I know where everything is." However true that may or not be, a cluttered, disorganized workspace gives the appearance of someone who is disorganized and disinterested in their work. This is not to say that you have to be one of those who are so organized that in their zeal for organization they lose focus on the job at hand. Remember, your job is to get the work done, not to organize a desk.

Somewhere between a total slob and a neat freak you will find a good common goal for your workspace. However, I would suggest being a bit closer to the neat freak. Very often, you will have to spend a little of your own money to achieve some order. For misguided reasons, companies are often reluctant to spend money on office supplies, especially organization supplies for entry level employees. In your early employment, you will likely find your colleagues utilizing discarded cardboard boxes to hold files as they are working on them, pens and pencils scattered across desks, and sometimes floors for lack of a holder, and files stacked on desks with little system to distinguish between work that is complete, and work that is not. All of this disorder will lead to missed deadlines and overlooked work.

If your company will purchase proper file cabinets and desk organization material, consider yourself lucky and acquire what you need and can. However, if like many companies they do not, be prepared to spend a little money. I am really talking about $200 or less. Get a small 2 to 3 drawer filing cabinet so that you may keep files that you are working on or use for reference close at hand and organized. Personally, I am a fan of dark wood tones or black as they tend to blend with almost all standard office décor. In addition, make sure you keep your files clearly labeled. The Avery Dennison Corporation supplies an entire line of labels that are remarkably easy to set up and use with almost any computer and printer. I also suggest using hanging files, as they will keep your working files from being crumpled or sliding underneath others and getting lost.

Purchase a decent desk set. This will give you a padded area for writing, and signing your name. Good desk sets will come with a pen/pencil holder so that you can keep these items neatly stored and at hand. Try to choose a desk set that has corresponding IN and OUT boxes so that you can keep your daily work organized. As silly as it sounds, supervisors will view your personal expenditures as a sign that you take yourself and your job seriously. These few little touches will easily set you apart from your less organized colleagues. Even if your performance is not particularly superior, your supervisors will notice your efforts towards organization and will perceive your work in a favorable light.

> *"...trend towards minimal and tasteful, and keep the smug sayings out of the office."*

Almost all of you will spend much of your working day utilizing a computer, and undoubtedly find this talk of files and IN boxes archaic. However, you will be surprised at just how much paperwork is involved, even in a modern office. But these organizational concerns do bring up the matter of keeping your computer organized as well. Like keeping a messy desk or office, keeping a messy desktop on your computer is just as confusing, and problematic. You will see people who will have dozens of documents, files and folders saved in no apparent order on their computer desktop. Much like a disorganized workspace, a disorganized computer desktop will also lead to confusion, lost work and missed deadlines.

Unlike a physical workspace however, it cost you no money to organize your computer. Create folders that are well labeled. Give your files accurate names, and make sure you include the date you created or last modified them in the file name. Take every precaution to make sure you back up your files, and if your company allows you to save and take files home, do so at the end of each week. All it takes is a small fire or a large electrical storm at the office, and a whole bunch of work is wiped out. If you are able to come in the next day with some backup files, your career has just taken off.

In addition to keeping your desk and work organized, keep your desk, cubicle or office neat and devoid of inappropriate personal items. Some people, especially a Type A boss, may swear by a sterile work space, completely devoid of any personal touches. At the other extreme there are people whose workspace is a veritable carnival of pictures, drawings, nick knacks and smug, assumed to be clever sayings along the lines of, "If I am ignoring you, assume you are wrong." I recommend leaning towards keeping a sterile workspace. A few pictures of your spouse or children are almost always acceptable. Examples of your children's artwork also add a personal, but not inappropriate warmth to your work environment. A small memento from your college, even a few pictures of places or scenes that you enjoy all help to make your workspace personal. I would strongly suggest that you trend towards minimal and tasteful, and keep the smug sayings out of the office.

In the same vein of keeping your workspace neat and organized, make sure you keep any projects or assignments you submit neat and organized. Never send anything, e-mail, memo, report, etc... until you have run it through spell checker and read it through one more time. Make sure your margins are uniform across your projects, and make sure your printer has plenty of toner or ink, depending on what your printer uses. Nothing can ruin a supervisor's perception of your work faster than streaks and faded parts throughout the project. Remember, your work is largely how your supervisors, and their supervisors will judge your performance. Take as much care and pride in getting it right as you can.

# CHAPTER 5
# HOW TO IMPRESS YOUR BOSS
♠♠♠♠
## (DON'T MESS IT UP NOW!)

Even a cursory glance at any management book will contain the concept of "Type A" vs. "Type B" personality types. In a work place setting, Type A individuals tend to be hard charging. They come in very early, tend to stay very late, work weekends, holidays, skip vacations and in doing so will get more work done than most and will be promoted faster. Therefore, unless you are or adopt a Type A personality you will eventually end up working for someone who is.

By and large, most people tend to be Type B personalities. In a work place setting, Type B individuals come to work on time, do not leave early, they will do solid but not exceptional work, and they will spend weekends, holidays and vacations with their friends and family. In general Type B personalities tend to report a higher quality of life. They have fewer heart attacks at 50, fewer divorces and closer relationships with their children. Never the less, you also have to figure out how to get along with your hard charging Type A boss.

I have had more than a few conversations with confirmed Type A managers who often make morbid jokes about early heart attacks and divorce. Type A managers often spend small fortunes on material goods in an effort to make it up to their spouses and children. Very often Type A managers lament the fact that they just cannot seem to help themselves. I had one person tell me with a mixture of both pride and sorrow about how they often come into the office on Christmas Day. As he stressed, "Well after the presents are opened and we have had lunch, there wasn't really much else for me to do, so I came on down to the office." Many Type A managers know they are crazy. However, the fact remains that often they are the ones who end up in charge. Hence, all others will have to adjust their work habits so as not to annoy the Type A boss.

*"...work is not like school. There is no extra credit..."*

Nothing will get you fired faster than coming to work late and/or leaving early on a regular basis. Crazy or not, Type A managers who have been at work since 5:00am will not understand why you came in at 8:15! Once or twice in a year they might accept, but once or twice a week, every week and they will fire you within months. In the same vein, Type A managers who often eat dinner at their desk night after night will not accept your leaving at 4:50 to "Beat the traffic!" Leave early more than once or twice a year and you could end up spending a lot of unplanned time at home.

The advice I give to all of my students is simple. Plan to be at work no later than 7:30am and leave no sooner than 6:00pm. Planning to be at work for these hours will have two very real benefits in improving your working relationship with a Type A supervisor. First, by working from 7:30 – 6:00, you are not coming in late or leaving early. By coming in a little early and leaving a little late you are making some effort to adjust to your supervisors working habits, and it will be noticed. In addition, by planning to be at work 30 minutes early, you will have extra time to deal with any unplanned emergencies, alarm did not go off, blown tire, stalled traffic etc, and will be less likely to show up after the start of business. Secondly, most people arrive at work no sooner than 5 minutes before they have to, and leave as soon as they can. By coming in a little early and leaving a little late, you will set yourself apart from almost everyone else you work with. Remember, much like when you were trying to set yourself apart from the other applicants when you were initially seeking employment, you are now competing with your coworkers for advancement.

As a side benefit of coming a little early and leaving a little late, you will spend a lot less time in traffic. A 30 minute drive to work if you leave at 7:30am will probably be a 10 minute drive if you leave at 7:15am. The same is true for the trip home. You have got to admit that less time in traffic, less gas wasted, and a better working relationship with your boss has got to be worth a little extra time out of your day.

In the same vein of getting along with a hard charging Type A boss, make sure you get ALL of your work done correctly and on time. A supervisor who is working long hours to get extra work done will not be understanding of anyone who cannot get their minimum assignments completed on time. Whatever you do, don't be late. You have to remember that work is not like school. There is no extra credit to make up for anything, or points taken off for late assignments. If you don't get your work done correctly and on time you will be fired. I tell all of my students to aim for getting their work done early. If you have a one week project that is due on Friday, get it done on Thursday. That gives you a whole day on Friday in case something goes wrong, or to polish your project before sending it up the line. The same holds true for longer assignments. Type A supervisors love work completed early, and they will remember.

# CHAPTER 6
# NETWORKING OUTSIDE THE WORKPLACE
♠♠♠♠
## (DO I HAVE TO WEAR THE HAT?)

It is in your best interests to get along with your boss. I would even go so far as to suggest that you need to actively cultivate a personal relationship with your supervisors. However, you need to be really careful not to let your efforts and desires to become personally friendly with your supervisors turn you into a kiss ass. No one, not even the boss, respects a kiss ass. "Great joke boss, let me get the door boss, do you need another drink boss, etc..." Don't be the office fool, but don't be the office opposition either.

By and large, the easiest and most respectable way to get along with your boss is to be good at your job. Come in a bit early, leave a bit late, get your work done on time and done right and you will have already set yourself apart from many of the people you are working with. However, aside from just getting along with your immediate supervisor, you need to be thinking and planning your long term career goals.

Pay some attention to what your boss, and more importantly what other people up the management chain consider important. If you work for a company where all the managers play golf, learn to play golf. I don't care if you think golf is silly, hate the outdoors, would rather do anything on a weekend but play, learn to play golf anyway. You don't have to be great, but when the invitation comes, be ready to keep up. Besides, you might really learn to like playing golf.

Likewise, if your upper level managers belong to any service or social clubs, Kiwanis, Masons, Junior League etc., then join, and join early. Don't come in and try to be too intimate with upper lever managers. They probably do not know you from work yet, and might become uncomfortable with your efforts to establish immediate rapport. Join and be active. However, maintain a respectful distance and give your supervisors a chance to notice and approach you.

Even though these organizations may be social and engage in volunteer work, always remember that you are actively seeking to build a good personal as well as professional rapport with your upper level managers. Go to the meetings often. Make sure you volunteer to help with any special projects the organization undertakes. Make sure that you do the best job you can, even if it is volunteer work. You are far more likely to work with upper level managers on a volunteer project long before your advancement through your job brings you into their circle. Let your supervisors see your best efforts. Just like on the job, the easiest way to gain the respect of your supervisors is to earn it through hard and competent work.

Have a good time. Most of these organizations are wonderfully fun, and you will meet a broad age group of people who have similar interests and goals. There are likely to be several eager recent college graduates like yourself. You may very well make long term acquaintances and even friends whom you will work and interact with throughout your career.

# CHAPTER 7
# MAINTAIN A PROFESSIONAL
# RELATIONSHIP WITH YOUR COWORKERS
♠♠♠♠
### (IT'S FIVE O'CLOCK SOMEWHERE)

Consider the friends that you have made from college, high school, from teams you may have been on, organizations you may have joined. Many of us have old and dear friends we have known for years and whom we trust and cherish. Be thankful for your friends. They will be a source of comfort and assistance over the years.

In an earlier chapter, we discussed the fact that in most workplace settings there will be you, 5 – 6 coworkers, and one supervisor. In all of your dealings with your coworkers keep in mind that you and your colleagues are all striving for promotion. You have to accept that not all of the people you work with will be your friends. Always remember that some of the people who are friendly to your face may be trying to get you in trouble behind your back. This is not to say that you will not find true and good friends at work. Some of my best friends have been made at work. However, always keep in mind that you are all competing for promotion, and guard your actions accordingly.

Whatever you do, NEVER complain about your boss, your job, your company or your work when you are with your coworkers. Whining and complaining about work is very common. Every job has its stresses and you will likely have frustrations that you would like to vent. However, you must keep in mind that the people you work with are also trying to get promoted.

> **"How effectively can you control and supervise a group of people who think you are a drunken buffoon?"**

In many instances, you will have coworkers who smile in your face, and then tell your supervisor all the negative complaining things you may say. The sad reality is that some people find that one of the easiest ways to get ahead is to take a few coworkers out at the knees.

However, backstabbing coworkers to get ahead is rarely effective for a long term career. No one, including your supervisors really trusts a deceptive person, and will not likely continue to promote such devious people. I suggest that you be a person of character who will always take the high road. In the long run, good personal character will be a career asset.

No one likes a complainer. No one likes to have someone insult them behind their back. A few poorly chosen words can effectively kill your career if they are reported back to your supervisor. I would recommend that you say nothing about your boss, or anyone for that matter, that you have not said to their face first. In fact, unless you have a serious complaint, I would strongly suggest that you keep all complaining to yourself. If you absolutely have to vent about work, talk to your parents, siblings, friends from school, just don't complain about work to anyone from work.

In the same spirit of keeping some distance from your coworkers, do not get drunk with the people from work. This is not to say that you don't go out for a drink or two after work, or meet for a ball game or any number of social events that you will likely engage in with coworkers. I am merely advocating that you do not get drunk or act stupid with your coworkers. For one reason, if you get drunk, you are far more likely to say or do something inappropriate that could get you in trouble at work, or even fired. I had one supervisor who lost his job over some drunken groping of coworkers, and even licking, yes licking, the back of a vice president's teenage daughter at a company Christmas party. We never actually saw that supervisor again. Also keep in mind that you are hoping to supervise these same coworkers in the future. Think of some of the drunken silly things you may have done in college, and the friends you have who remember some of your antics. How effectively can you control and supervise a group of people who think you are a drunken buffoon? Learn to have one or two drinks at most. Have fun, but don't get drunk and silly with your coworkers and make sure you leave at a decent hour. If you still like to drink to excess and party hard, go back to your old college town and have a great time. People from school are your friends; people from work are your competition. Learn to keep them separate.

# CHAPTER 8
# PRO'S AND CON'S OF DATING AT WORK
♠♠♠♠
## (BREAKING UP IS HARD TO DO)

Most of you reading this book have had boyfriends or girlfriends, you may even be dating someone right now. However, think back over your dating life and you are also likely remember past boyfriends or girlfriends. Most people who are graduating from college have dated several people over the past few years. In doing so, you have also been forced to break up for various reasons. Regardless of the reason, breaking up is very hard to do. In most cases, feelings are hurt, insults are hurled, and one or both of you are angry, sometimes bitter. Now imagine that after going through a hard difficult break up, you will have to come to work on Monday, indeed every weekday for the near future and be forced to work with your ex for eight to ten hours a day, five days a week. If you have ever experienced the pain and awkwardness of seeing an ex around campus, running into them at a party etc, imagine the difficulty of working with them for hours a day, day after day after day. Now you understand why it is recommended that you not date people from your workplace.

I personally have mixed feelings about recommending that you not date coworkers. Obviously it would cause problems when and if you break up. However, it is also possible that you may find someone at work with whom you will fall in love, marry and live a long and happy life. This is not all that improbable when you consider that you both have a lot in common, merely by the fact that you choose the education career and employment decisions that brought you to the same company. Therefore, it is not unlikely that you will find people that you are attracted to on more than a physical level.

To address this issue, I often recommend that people take a few steps. First and foremost, take it very slow. If your attraction is purely physical, leave it alone. In the event that you break up, one or both of you will likely have to leave. Frankly, pure physical attraction, though not without its merits, should not be a reason to interfere with your career. However, if after working with someone for some time, you find that aside, or in addition to anything physical, you like and are attracted to them for deeper reasons, do consider starting a relationship.

However, I have a couple of warnings if you choose to date someone from work. First and foremost, if one of you is supervising the other, then someone needs to change jobs or departments before you date, and certainly before you date very long. Most companies have rather strict policies about dating subordinates, and it is not inconceivable that one or both of you may be fired if you date. In addition, other members in a department often resent any perception of preferential treatment you may give to the person you are dating as well as supervising. If you have taken the relationship slowly, and you both feel that this relationship may have some depth, then changing jobs or departments may be necessary

> **"Keep your dirty jokes, any pornography or inappropriate pictures at home."**

to accommodate your budding relationship. If you are no longer working together, and the relationship does not work out, you will also be spared the pain of being forced into close quarters while you nurse hurt feelings.

Another serious problem that arises from dating in the workplace is the concept of Sexual Harassment. Sexual harassment can take on many forms. The crudest form occurs when a supervisor offers or implies that they can help or hurt someone's career in exchange for sexual favors. To be clear, they do not have to ask for sexual acts in order to have committed sexual harassment. Constantly pressing for a date under the guise of discussing work place issues, "Lets talk about this over dinner at my place" for example can and will be considered sexual harassment. When you move into a supervisory role, NEVER seek to use that role to coerce someone into a date, much less sexual acts. It is probable that you will be fired; it is possible that you may go to jail.

By far the most common form of sexual harassment is termed, "Hostile Environment" sexual harassment. Hostile environment can be found in the workplace with such actions as sexual jokes in the hallways, pictures of nude or scantly clad individuals leaning over cars, on beds etc, pornography on someone's computer, inappropriate e-mails are all examples of hostile sexual behavior which can escalate to the level of sexual harassment. Keep your dirty jokes, any pornography or inappropriate pictures at home. At work, supervisor or not, maintain a professional demeanor.

In addition to inappropriate pictures, jokes or actions, hostile environment sexual harassment can also arise when a supervisor or a coworker keeps pressing someone for a date. The courts have ruled repeatedly that asking someone out for one date, especially if they are not married, is not considered sexual harassment. Regardless of whether you are a supervisor or merely a coworker, it is usually permissible to ask someone out once. Depending on their response, you may be able to ask a second time. If, when you ask the first time, they make it clear that they do not want to date you, then you need to back off. Statements along the lines of; "I don't like to date people I work with." or "I am dating someone." or especially something blunt in which they make it plain they do not wish to date you, have to be respected. Asking them out again and again will likely get you fired.

> "Work is not a bar or a college party..."

If they leave the option open for maybe a date in the future, perhaps something along the lines of; "I have a date this weekend, but maybe later." means you can ask them out once more. If they pass the second time, stop. If they are truly

41

interested, let them ask you. However, in most cases they are trying to let you down easily, and you need to take the hint. Work is not a bar or a college party in which you can follow someone around again and again. Work is a professional setting, and must be treated as such.

# CHAPTER 9
# ESSENTIAL ETHICAL CONCEPTS
# FOR THE WORKPLACE
♠♠♠♠
## (WHO ME?)

The concept of ethical organizational behavior has been revitalized of late, and many companies have strengthened their ethical guidelines as a result. It is essential that anyone entering the workplace understand some general ethical concepts. In addition, even as the focus on ethics may fade as time and new crisis take its place, there are some ethical concepts that are certainly helpful for a long prosperous career.

One of the core ideas of ethics that everyone needs to understand is the concept of professional ethics. Many professions require certain actions or behaviors of their members that may or may not seem proper to those outside of the profession. One of the best examples of professional ethics is to consider the obligations of lawyers under the United States legal system. In the United States, indeed in much of the countries colonized by Great Britain, lawyers are required to engage in a combative contest in the search for justice. Lawyers are required to argue their clients position, and compete to get the best result for their client. This often leads to arguments of innocent, in spite of being found burying the body, and apparently guilty individuals are sometimes set free with the assistance of a talented lawyer. When you wonder why an attorney would strive so hard to free an apparently guilty person, you have to remember that they are required to do so by the professional ethical requirements of their chosen career.

> "...if you have to wait until no one is watching before you do something at work, then you should not do it."

In addition to attorneys, many other professions also require professional ethical decisions that are sometimes difficult to those who must abide by them. For example, accountants have very strict guidelines for the recording and reporting of an organization's financial documents. Physicians have to balance the preferred level of a patient's treatment against the potential limits of practical medicine, along with the added burden of contending with the after action lawsuits. As a teacher, I have students who study hard or whom I like personally only to find that they are not always successful in the classroom. It is often emotionally draining for me to assign these students the grades they have earned, as opposed to the grades they desire. However, as a professional educator, it is inappropriate to alter one student's grades and leave other students' grades to merit. Much like a teacher, supervisors will have employees whom they like personally, or employees who will try hard without success. It will be difficult and emotionally draining for the supervisor to discipline or dismiss people who are not successful despite their desires. However, from a professionally ethical standpoint, it would be inappropriate to evaluate a few employees personally, and others by merit. It will not always be easy to be the boss, it really is lonely at the top. However if you hold to one established standard, you will be fair and ethical in your dealings with coworkers.

In addition to professional ethics, and much harder to specify is the concept of personal ethics. As the name implies, personal ethics will vary from individual to individual. National or religious backgrounds, early home life, personal and educational experiences will all combine within an individual to establish a personal set of ethical and moral codes. These personal ethical codes will vary among individuals. Therefore, individuals will have different degrees of acceptance for somewhat questionable actions. For example, most people would consider the theft of a laptop computer from the workplace an unethical action. Fewer individuals might consider the removal of a $3.00 pack of paper from the workplace to be unethical, and fewer still would consider the removal of a single $1.00 pen to be unethical. However, there are also individuals who would consider the removal of any office supply unethical, unless it was taken specifically for company use. If as you read this example and you find yourself wondering which position is correct, then you now see the dilemma of personal ethics.

To use the previous example, most of us would agree that stealing a computer is unethical. However, I carry a pen with me most of the time and often forget to leave my pen at work. From time to time, I make an effort to round up my ill-gotten loot and return them to my desk, but in reality there are about five or six pilfered pens scattered from my office to car to home. As the value of the pens in question is small, my removal is inadvertent, and I make no effort to hide my actions, I do not consider my wandering pen collection unethical. However, there are others who would disagree.

Most organizations have guidelines that do not allow the taking of office supplies, or any other equipment for personal use. In practice, organizations do vary in their enforcement of this rule. However, as a general guideline, I would suggest that little if any removal of company supplies is acceptable, as this can be construed as theft.

I advise all of my students to do nothing in the workplace that you could not do right in front of your boss. My wandering pen collection not withstanding, unless you do considerable work for your company at home, I do not recommend taking company supplies from work. I would also strongly advise against trying to do a second job for someone else while at your regular workplace. Making photocopies for yourself that is not job related, or for your spouse or children's projects is also generally frowned upon. If in doubt, consider that if you have to wait until no one is watching before you do something at work, then you should not do it.

However, there is a big twist in the whole ethical advice that I give to my students. Make sure that you do not get caught between your company and the law. If a company is suspected of illegal activities, very often the investigation will begin by targeting people who hold entry level or slightly higher college level jobs.

Something like an Annual Report, which is filed with the Securities and Exchange Commission every year, can be altered relatively easily. However, the sheer number of lower and midlevel college graduate positions, and the volume of information generated by these positions would make it difficult if not impossible for the company to coordinate a deception in the face of an investigation. When faced with an investigation, some unethical managers will often ask individuals in these lower and midlevel college graduate positions to alter, erase or otherwise destroy copies of the work and reports that have been submitted. If you know, or even suspect that your company is under investigation, NEVER alter, erase or otherwise destroy anything. If you are asked to do so by your boss, insist on getting that instruction in writing. It is doubtful that your supervisor will give you an illegal or unethical order in writing, and it is more than a remote possibility that you will be fired for refusing to alter, erase or destroy your files. I strongly suggest that if you find yourself in this situation that you make copies of as many of your documents as you can, and keep them hidden. In the event that something happens to your computer or files, "by accident" or you are fired and your work is altered or deleted in your absence, you will need copies of the original files to keep from being blamed and possibly prosecuted for destroying evidence. The sad reality is that young junior level employees are easily prosecuted for altering or destroying evidence in the face of an investigation. Therefore, DO NOT erase or alter your documents, and protect yourself if you find yourself in this situation. Although you may lose your job, that is far better than going to jail.

# CHAPTER 10
# SOME ADVICE ON INSURANCE
♠♠♠♠
## (IT'S NOT ALL ABOUT THE LIZARD)

Many of you are already familiar with automotive insurance. At the very minimum, I suggest you carry liability insurance to protect yourself from lawsuits in the event of an accident. You will probably need to carry some collision insurance to cover the value of your car in case of an accident. In addition, I strongly suggest you consider some roadside assistance coverage, either with your insurance company, or with a good national company such as the American Automobile Association (AAA). If you ever blow a tire or have engine failure in the middle of nowhere, you will be glad you have AAA.

One of the major advantages of completing a college degree is that you are now eligible for a job with benefits! I have a steady stream of students who stress that the desire for a good job with some benefits has been one of the major motivating factors for completing college. Various types of insurance are certainly one of the major benefits of having a good job.

When you mention the word insurance, most people immediately jump to Health Insurance, and with good reason.

Uninsured, a trip to the doctor for even a minor illness and the resulting prescription costs are often a few hundred dollars. Trips to the emergency room for relatively minor concerns, a broken arm comes to mind, can easily run into a few thousand dollars. Should something simple such as an appendix need to be removed you can top 10 – 20 thousand dollars very easily. Therefore, the desire for good health coverage is a major motivator for many people to complete college.

Many students are covered under their parents' plan during the time they are in college. If this is the case, especially if you have any ongoing health issues, then you need to make sure that this coverage lasts past graduation, and determine for how long. Coverage post graduation for three to six months is common. However coverage lasting for 30 days past graduation is becoming increasingly normal, and I have even known a few policies to stop the day of graduation. DO NOT go without insurance while you look for a job. Aside from the "you might get sick angle", the real concern

> "...you are going to find out that you got what you paid for with an HMO."

is that most insurance programs will not cover preexisting conditions if previous insurance coverage has lapsed. Your safest and cheapest method if you are faced with losing coverage is to purchase Major Medical insurance. Young single healthy graduates can easily purchase Major Medical coverage for $50 - $100 a month. If you are able to purchase coverage with the same company with which you insure a car, major medical insurance might even be slightly lower.

I strongly recommend that you use a large nation-wide insurance company as they are likely to have a good policy. Major Medical Insurance is different than what many of you think of as standard health insurance. As the name implies, "Major Medical" health insurance policies only cover major medical expenses. A typical policy only covers medical expenses after the first $10,000 - $20,000 dollars. Therefore, if you only have major medical health insurance, you will pay all the minor expenses of seeing a doctor for general health care. For example, if you get a head cold, you will pay a couple of hundred dollars to see a doctor and get a prescription filled. However, if you already have any preexisting medical issues, or if something catastrophic such as a severe car accident, you are diagnosed with cancer, or any number of concerns should arise while you are between school and employment, you will be facing medical bills of only thousands of dollars as opposed to hundreds of thousands of dollars. In addition, any lingering effects or long term care would be covered under your new health insurance policy when you start to work.

When you begin your new job, if at all possible avoid HMO Medical coverage. HMO's make it sound so good, and it is going to be hard to avoid the HMO sales pitch. First and foremost, HMO health insurance is going to be cheaper than full coverage health insurance. The monthly rate for HMO health insurance will be cheaper. HMO's will talk about $20 co pays at the doctor, $10 prescription rates, and it seems so reasonable to agree to follow their rules and guidelines for treatment in exchange for the lower cost. To be completely honest, as long as you remain healthy, with maybe a head cold once or twice a year, HMO coverage is great, and is certainly cheaper then full coverage insurance. However, should something go wrong, car accident, cancer etc., you are going to find out that you got what you paid for with an HMO. A restriction such as, "Two X-rays a year" is no problem when you have a head cold. However, a major car accident with leg, arm, rib and back injuries will call for multiple x-rays, all costing $300 - $500, and if you have a restrictive HMO policy, you will pay for every one of them starting with the third x-ray.

If it is available, I personally recommend Blue Cross and Blue Shield health insurance, or any insurance policy that lets you choose your own physicians. I will readily admit that full coverage health insurance will be more expensive than the HMO plans. You will have higher deductibles, full coverage insurance often pays 80% of your expenses while you pay the remaining 20%. I will also admit that in most years full coverage health insurance will cost you more. However, if you follow the news at all, you will see that people sue their HMO providers on a regular basis for denied care. Very often someone has died as the result of this denied care. If anything serious arises, you will be glad that you have chosen full coverage health insurance. In doing so, you will get the care prescribed by a physician, and not an accountant.

One of the most overlooked forms of insurance, especially with young college graduates, is Disability Insurance. In brief, disability insurance will pay either a percentage of your salary or a set monthly amount that begins in the event you are injured and unable to continue working. Hopefully this is insurance you will never have to claim. However, over the years you will likely to be purchasing homes, cars, getting married and having children, and all of these activities, especially children, will require almost all of your income in order to sustain your life style. A car accident that results in a head injury, neck or back injuries that result in paralysis, any number of illnesses can leave you permanently disabled and unable to work. Unfortunately, I personally know of a former student of mine who on a college graduation trip contracted viral encephalitis. Instead of beginning medical school that fall, he now lives in a full time care facility for the

> "...the minute someone gets pregnant, you will need to revise your life insurance policies."

mentally disabled.  Scary or not, sometimes things go wrong, and you have to plan for them.

However, especially for college graduates, there are ways to reduce the cost of disability insurance.  One of the ways to reduce your disability insurance costs is to accept a lower percentage of your salary in case you are disabled.  Most policies allow you to choose from as little as 40% to as much as 80% and sometimes 100% of your income.  My personal advice is to choose either the highest percentage or monthly dollar amount that you can.  Granted it will cost a bit more for the insurance, but in the event that you are permanently disabled, you will likely have ongoing medical expenses, and you will need all the money you can get.

The best way to lower the cost of disability insurance, especially for college graduates, is to adjust WHEN your disability insurance will start to pay your salary.  Many professions such as construction or truck driving would prevent someone with relatively minor injuries, a broken leg comes to mind, from working.  Individuals performing such physical jobs would need disability insurance that would kick in quickly, as such injuries are likely to prevent them from working.  However, most college graduate jobs can easily accommodate individuals with broken legs, ribs, arms etc. Granted you may need a week off to let things settle down, but you do not have to wait for the bones to heal before returning to your desk job. Disability insurance that starts immediately is expensive. However, if you choose a policy that only starts to pay in one, three, or even six months after you are injured, you will likely cost half as much, maybe even a quarter of the cost of immediate disability insurance. Consider what is required for your job, weigh any support that you can expect from your family, and the needs you may have for yourself and any spouse or children you may have. If you can count on some support for a few months, then press the start date for your disability out to at least three, and I recommend six months. It will cost a lot less for disability insurance, and carry minimal long term risks.

Most of you have seen ads on TV touting the need to purchase Life Insurance now, before it is too late. Remember, like any company, life insurance companies are trying to sell you something. Unless something catastrophic happens, it is almost never too late to purchase life insurance, WHEN YOU NEED IT. It is important to keep in mind the main purpose for life insurance. In brief, life insurance replaces your income so that those who depend on you for their support will be able to survive in the event you die. Generally, unless you have children, you do not need life insurance.

Most college graduate jobs will offer some form of either free or almost free life insurance. There is nothing wrong with $10 - $20 dollars a month for the around $100,000 in coverage that these baseline policies generally provide. As long as you do not have children, this will cover all of your responsibilities. In the event that you die, $100,000 would allow your spouse or parents to provide you a decent funeral. Money would be available to clear any outstanding debts, and in the case that you are married, this money would give your spouse some time to adjust to the loss of your income.

However, the minute someone gets pregnant, you will need to revise your life insurance policies. Children are expensive. They will require medical care, food, clothing, shelter, some toys and all sorts of other expenses for 18 – 20 years at least. If you consider the cost of a college education for your children, then you should clearly see that $100,000 is not sufficient to meet your obligations.

In a later chapter we will discuss the benefits of retirement planning. In that chapter, we will discuss the need to save enough money so that when you retire, your savings will generate enough interest to replace your income. When considering your life insurance needs, especially when you have children, you have to take out enough life insurance so that your family will immediately have enough insurance money so that the interest it earns will replace most of your income.

Most people get this wrong. They take out $500,000, maybe even $1,000,000 and think they are fine. However, money that your family will need to live on in the event that you have died has to be invested conservatively. Therefore, your family can only expect a 6% to maybe 8% rate of return on this money. In addition, you have to plan to reinvest 3% of the money earned each year to offset inflation. Therefore, keep in mind that a $1,000,000 life insurance policy will only replace about $40,000 - $50,000 of your income a year.

Most people, especially people in professional occupations will need to periodically review their insurance coverage to make sure that they adequately protect their family in the event of an untimely death. If you are earning around

$100,000 a year, then you will probably need around $1,500,000 to $2,000,000 in life insurance to keep your family in the home, schools and lifestyle that they knew before you were gone.

Many companies will allow you to arrange for a life insurance policy of $500,000 to maybe as much as a $1,000,000 either through them, or more likely with an outside insurance company which has made arrangements with your workplace. This will most likely be your least expensive option for life insurance, and you should take out the most you can there first. However, you will likely need to take out a second policy outside of work for perhaps $1,000,000 or more with another insurance company. I strongly recommend that you go to a large nationwide insurance company for your policy. In addition, having an independent life insurance policy will provide your family some protection in the event you lose or leave your present job.

Life insurance comes in many forms. The agent will talk about policies that allow you to build equity, maybe even talk about life insurance as a retirement saving option. However, the worst rate of return for any retirement savings will be through an insurance company. What you want is something called "Term" life insurance. Term life insurance will insure you for a set number of years, usually from 10 to maybe 25 years. You will pay the same monthly fee every year for the term of the policy, and if you do not die before the term ends, you get nothing back. However, term life insurance is by far the cheapest option to get the maximum coverage you need. I recommend that you take out the longest term life insurance policy the insurance company will offer, usually 20 – 25 years. Remember your children will hopefully be going to college and that means you need insurance until they are 22 – 25 at least. In general, a $1,000,000 to $1,500,000 policy for someone who is relatively healthy will cost about $100 - $150 a month for the entire length of the policy. Remember, your children are helpless, and you have to make sure to protect them.

# CHAPTER 11
# SAVING FOR RETIREMENT
♠♠♠♠
## (THAT NEW CAR WILL COST YOU
## OVER A MILLION DOLLARS)

One of the overlooked realities of starting a new job is that the sooner you start to save for retirement the better off you will be. That is a hard concept for people who just got their first job to grasp, but at some point you will want to stop going to work. The sooner you plan for retirement the more money you will have to retire on.

Over the years, I have had students tell me about how they are tired of roommates, tired of their car, TV, furniture, want an iPod etc. I know from personal experience that you look forward with eager anticipation to that first pay check. To anyone who has struggled through school, and worked hard for minimum wage, that first check seems like a fortune, and we have all heard the call of commerce. Let us be clear, I am not saying not to spend any money on a desired item, but a little caution and a little restraint will result in far more money than you expect.

The secret to not being dead broke your whole life is to get some money into the bank soon. Money that has been saved will earn some interest. Money that has been invested will likely earn some profit. Any money put away will work for you over time. If you manage to get $10,000 saved. It will likely earn you an extra $1000 the following year. Think about that, an extra $1000 and you did not have to work to get it. Imagine how much fun it will be when you get some real money working for you.

The best way to save for retirement is to put money into some form of tax free retirement account. Anyone with a job can put up to $5000 a year into something called an Individual Retirement Account (IRA). Many companies will also have some form of retirement plan, either something called a 401(k) or a 403(b) depending on the type of organization for which you work. In addition, many companies will match money you place into a retirement account, at least up to a certain point. ALWAYS PUT

> *"...this is the concept that could keep you from working at Wal-Mart when you are in your sixties."*

MONEY INTO AN ACCOUNT THAT YOUR COMPANY WILL MATCH! They are basically giving you free money, and all you have to do is agree not to spend everything you make. Most companies will match somewhere around $1500 to $2000 and if you are lucky, maybe a bit more. Basically you only put $2000 of your salary into a retirement account, but at the end of the year you have an account with $4000 in it. And if you do the same thing next year, you will add another $4000 to it. Can you see how this might get exciting? I would advise you to not put all your money and retirement hopes into just one plan, especially the company plan. Figure that you should give up $4000 - $5000 a year out of your own money for every year you are in your twenties. Put the maximum into your company plan that they will give you matching money for, and put the rest into an IRA.

I know, I know! We are talking about taking $100 a week out of your hard earned money, and I know you do not make all that much in the beginning, but let me show you it is worth it.

Earlier we talked about how money that has been put aside will probably earn you some money if it is left alone. The example was where $10,000 will earn you an extra $1000 if you leave it alone for a year. This is a concept called growth and interest. Now for a really fun concept, in the following year you not only earn another $1000, but you will also earn an extra $100 on the $1000 you earned from last year's savings. Each additional year, you could earn the $1000 on the original $10,000 and an extra $100 a year for each year you leave it alone. This is called compound interest, and this is the concept that could keep you from working at Wal-Mart when you are in your sixties.

Money earning around 10% a year will double about every seven years. That means if you get $10,000 saved away by the time you are 23 (usually two years after graduation) that original $10,000 will be worth $20,000 when you are 30. It will be worth $40,000 when you are 37. It will be worth $80,000 when you are 44. It's starting to sound fun about now, right? It will be worth $160,000 when you are 51. It will be worth $320,000 when you are 58. Wait for it, wait for it! When you get to be 65 years old and are good and sick of going to work, that $10,000 you did not waste on stuff when you were young will be worth around $640,000. And here is the really fun part. This was on money you saved before you were 23! If you get a second $10,000 saved by the time you are 25, it will be worth an additional $640,000 when you are 67. EVERY $10,000 you get saved in your twenties will be worth about $640,000 when you want to retire. Likewise, EVERY $10,000 you do not save in your twenties will cost you around $640,000 when you are old and sick and don't want to get up in the mornings anymore.

How can someone find an extra $5,000 a year out of their pay check? The worst mistake you can make when you gradate from college is to rush out and buy a new car. Even a used new car will cost you a fortune in lost savings. I have heard all the reasons about unreliable, breaks all the time, funny noises, etc.... Most of the time your car is just fine. Granted you may

> "How bad can those feet be?"

spend some money from time to time to repair it. However, unless you have blown the transmission or the engine and they are talking about three to four thousand dollars to repair your car, it is better to fix it and keep on driving. Even a modest car, something around $15,000 - $20,000 will cost you five to six thousand dollars a year, EVERY year for the next five years of your life. Remember every $10,000 you do not save in your 20's will cost you around $640,000 in lost savings when you reach retirement. Stick with your old car for at least two or three years. You are going to get raises. If you are wise, you will put the extra money into savings until you absolutely have to buy a new car. In addition, your raises will probably increase your take home pay by three to four hundred dollars a month in a few years and you can now have retirement savings, and a good car.

Another big mistake is to rush out and live alone. Granted, living in a dorm was rough, and maybe you are sick and tired of roommates, their friends, having to share the TV etc.... But are you so sick of roommates that you would literally give up a million dollars or so that you could earn with the money you save from shared expenses? Keep in mind that if you have a roommate, you are only responsible for half the rent and half the utilities. If you only save three to four hundred dollars a month from having a roommate, that comes out to about $4,000 to $5,000 a year in savings. There is your retirement money right there. Maybe you don't like your roommate, maybe their feet do stink, but you really are talking about giving up over a million dollars every two years you choose to live alone. How bad can those feet be?

# CHAPTER 12
# THINKING ABOUT LONG TERM CAREERS
## ♠♠♠♠
## (BUT I JUST GOT A JOB)

Once you have found employment, organized your financial and insurance needs and have begun the process of learning and succeeding at your job, most people find themselves wondering, "Now what?" It may not come as a surprise to those of you who have been reading this book that I do have some advice to help guide you as you seek and settle onto a career path.

You must keep in mind that there is a big difference between a job and a career. A "Job" is what you happen to be doing at the moment in order to earn money. Most of my students have had several jobs along the years. Maybe you started with babysitting or yard work. Many of you have held low paying hourly wage jobs before and during college. Even the hopefully better paying position you get when you graduate from college is a job.

In contrast, a career is a long term plan in which you consider the money you wish to earn, the jobs you are willing to undertake to earn this money, and the hours you are willing to sacrifice at work for the lifestyle you desire. As I am sure you are aware, some professions pay better than others. With rare

> "Many graduate programs are tailored to working professionals, and will offer courses in the evening, weekends and sometimes online."

exception, the professions that pay better require longer and often more difficult graduate studies, and/or longer and more difficult working hours and conditions. Most college graduates will spend several years after graduation weighing their desires for more money against the requirements they will have to fulfill to earn more money.

I usually advise my students to try and determine where they would like to be in life when they are 30 – 35 years old. Don't be overly concerned with trying to determine where you want to be at the end of your career. Remember, many of you are still getting started on a career path, and will be getting started for the next couple of years. Once you have found your balance of career and life goals, then you will have a better understanding of your options for the next 30 – 40 years. However, I stress to my students the need to focus on what you would like to be doing and how you would like to be living when you get to your mid-thirties. This thought process will help you determine what steps you have to take over the next few years to successfully achieve your long term goals.

I always advise my students to not choose a career based solely on money. As you are considering career options, keep in mind that whatever path you choose, you will be at work for 40 – 50 hours a week, 48 weeks a year for 40 years of your only life. Please remember, if you choose a career that involves work that you do not enjoy, then you could live a miserable life. Every job will have requirements that you may not enjoy. Every job will have its bad days, even bad weeks. However, if you choose a profession that means you dislike going to work almost every day, you will be unhappy almost every day.

I stress to my students that almost every professional level job has the potential to   pay about $40,000 to $50,000 dollars a year when you reach your mid-thirties. This level of income will provide a very solid and stable standard of living for yourself, and a family. Granted you will drive a Ford instead of a Mercedes, your home may be smaller than the surgeons, but you will have plenty of money for your needs such as food, clothing and shelter, as well as many of your wants. In addition, if you are not miserable when you come home from work, you will have a much better life with your family and friends.

In order to make $40,000 to $50,000 a year, or more, you may very well have to go back to college for one or two years in order to get a graduate degree. Some organizations provide tuition reimbursement to their employees who seek advanced education. Many of these organizations offer the tuition money with little or no restrictions. However, it is not unusual for an organization to require you to refund any tuition money that they have provided you if you voluntarily leave their employment before two or three years has passed after graduating with your advanced degree. Make sure you clearly understand, and are willing to accept any reimbursement requirements before you accept your organization's tuition money. If you feel that you would like to continue with your organization for a few years, tuition reimbursement is a great way to further your education at little personal cost. Many graduate programs are tailored to working professionals, and will offer courses in the evening, weekends and sometimes online. These options should allow you to continue working full time while you pursue your education. In almost all situations, advanced education enhances your career opportunities as well as demonstrating your willingness to do what it takes to succeed.

As you start to settle on a potential career path, seek out and meet with people who are already in the jobs and on the career paths you are considering. Take them to lunch and ask about their work. Probe them for information about what they perceive to be the pro's and con's of their professions. Get their advice on any graduate programs you may need to pursue, and what early jobs you should seek to prepare you to move into their professions. Do not ask them how much they make as this is almost always considered rude. Sometimes they may offer some general salary advice, but never ask.

As you are considering your career options, I would strongly suggest that you stay in your first post college job for at least a year. It is not unusual for people to change jobs three or four times post graduation while they are seeking a fulfilling career. Employers know this, and they often look for a steady progression in your employment history as you explore and hopefully narrow down your career choices. However, every time someone leaves a job, employers are forced to begin a search to find a replacement. Therefore, they do seek to hire people who they think will stay with the company for a while at least. If you change jobs every few months several times in a row employers may become very reluctant to hire you, as they will suspect that you will leave them shortly as well. Therefore, unless you really dislike your job, your boss, your surroundings etc, I would strongly suggest you not leave a job until you have been employed for at least one year.

It is not unusual for entry level jobs to be less than fulfilling. However, it is possible that you may find a potential career path within the organization you are working for if you take the time to consider your advancement options. Hopefully, you had some good reasons to choose to work for this organization in the first place. You may have to allow some time before you find your best fit within the organization. I do strongly recommend that you give your job and your organization at least a year. This will allow you sufficient time to discover and weigh your career options within the organization. Remember, you can always move on if you decide you would not be happy here, but do allow some time to make an informed decision.

Believe me when I tell you that I know looking for work and searching for a rewarding career can be frustrating, stressful and even a little embarrassing at times. However, I would assure you that if you work hard at your job, keep current with your education and manage your finances; a lot of the stresses in your personal and professional lives will lessen in time. I would encourage all of you to pursue your dreams, and I wish you all the best of luck with your endeavors.

Scott Kenneth Campbell holds a dual track PH.D from Auburn University in the fields of Human Resource Management and Organizational Analysis. For over a decade, Dr. Campbell has taught graduate and undergraduate courses at universities in both the United States of America, and in Europe. Over the years, he has assisted hundreds of students in their quest to find professional post-graduate employment.

Prior to pursuing a career in academics, Dr. Campbell was a broker with Morgan Stanley. Early in his working career, he was a consumer loan specialist with Regions Bank and he was also a corporate sales executive with Sprint PCS. In addition, he spent two years in Hungary as a Small Business Development Volunteer with the United States Peace Corps.

Dr. Campbell is a full time professor with the School of Business at Francis Marion University, in Florence, South Carolina where he resides with his wife and three wonderful daughters.

www.ingramcontent.com/pod-product-compliance
Lightning Source LLC
Chambersburg PA
CBHW070911280326
41934CB00008B/1671